T0246942

THE EXODUS

Rose Visual
Bible Studies

R SE
PUBLISHING

The Exodus
Rose Visual Bible Studies

© 2024 Rose Publishing
Published by Rose Publishing
An imprint of Tyndale House Ministries
Carol Stream, Illinois
www.hendricksonrose.com

ISBN 978-1-4964-7976-1

Author: Danielle Parish, MDiv, Senior Pastor at Spark Church in Palo Alto, California

Printed in the United States of America
010324VP

Contents

"This is a day to remember forever—
the day you left Egypt,
the place of your slavery.
Today the LORD has brought you out
by the power of his mighty hand."

Exodus 13:3 NLT

The Exodus

In 2007 on the island of Crete in Greece, I had the good fortune to join a group of Jews gathering for the Passover. During World War II, the Jewish population of Crete was tragically destroyed, along with the synagogue in Hania. But this year, Jews and friends from all over the world came together on Crete to celebrate the restoration of the synagogue and to ensure that the Passover story would be told once again. Despite the Nazis' attempts to forever silence the narrative and the Jewish people, the Jews gathered to tell again the story of resistance and victory over evil. As I sat there listening to the exodus story retold in Greek, Hebrew, and English, I was so grateful for the resilience of a people and the wisdom of God's commands to remember the Passover.

Retelling a story of freedom year after year has a way ensuring that people never forget who they are—and who God is. As Christians, we retell our story of freedom from death and sin every Resurrection Sunday and every time we take Communion. The exodus story reaches back even further in the biblical story of God rescuing his creation. The book of Exodus tells of events that are foundational to the faith we read about in both the Old and the New Testaments.

In the story of the exodus, the people of Israel are enslaved in Egypt, wondering whether God's covenantal promises to Abraham will truly be fulfilled. Suffering under oppression and violence, they cry out, and God hears, remembers, and acts. Through miraculous signs and wonders, God warns Pharaoh to relent, delivers Israel by parting the sea, and brings the people to a mountainside in Sinai to make a covenant.

With your Bible in one hand and this study guide in the other, let us take an in-depth look at the story of the exodus, retelling an ancient story that reminds us of who we are and who our God is.

1

GOD HEARS

Israel in Egypt

God Hears

The Hebrew name for the book of Exodus is *Shemot,* which means "names." It is taken from the beginning of the first verse: "These are the names of the sons of Israel who went to Egypt with Jacob, each with his family" (Ex. 1:1). From the start, the writer of Exodus connects readers to the narratives about Israel's ancestors found in the book of Genesis. The writer assumes that we readers are intimately acquainted with the names and the stories of the patriarchs and matriarchs. Names like Abraham, Sarah, Isaac, Rebekah, Jacob, Leah, Rachel, Zilphah, Bilhah, Judah, and Joseph all bring to mind stories of heartache, betrayal, hope, and triumph.

In order to know where we are and where we are going, we need to know where we are from. The people and events in Genesis lay the foundation for what happens in the book of Exodus. In turn, the defining events of the exodus shape the identity of the people of God throughout the rest of the Bible.

Exodus is the telling of what was prophesied in Genesis: exile, slavery, deliverance, redemption, and, ultimately, a story about the God who hears his people and is faithful to his promises.

Read It

Key Bible Passage

For this session, read Genesis 15:1–21; 47:1–12 and Exodus 1:1–14.

Optional Reading

Genesis 12:1–9; 50:1–26

"They made their lives bitter with harsh labor in brick and mortar and with all kinds of work in the fields; in all their harsh labor the Egyptians worked them ruthlessly."

EXODUS 1:14

Know It

1. In Genesis 15, God blesses Abram and his descendants, but he also warns that four hundred years of slavery are coming. How would you respond to God after such news?

2. Compare the pharaoh in Genesis 47 to the new pharaoh in Exodus 1. What brought about such a dramatically different treatment of the Israelites?

3. Rather than focusing on characters like Abraham, Joseph, or Pharaoh, look again at the Bible passages and consider God as the central character. What do you notice when you focus on God's role in these narratives?

God Cuts a Deal

Genesis is not simply the story of a large family. It is the story of God's covenantal faithfulness to the world *through* that family.

In Genesis 15, Abram (later renamed Abraham), without children of his own, speaks to God for the first time, questioning God's faithfulness. God reassures Abram that indeed he will have descendants as numerous as the stars and they will live not as exiles, but in a land promised by God. Abram believes God and they "cut a deal." The Hebrew word for covenant-making (*berit*) literally translates "to cut" a covenant. While the cutting of animals and walking between the pieces is an odd concept to us, it was a familiar covenant-making practice that Abram would have understood (see Jer. 34:18–20). The same fate that befalls the animal will fall upon the person who violates the covenant. Whoever does not keep up their end of the covenant, this same cutting will be done to them. The smoking fire pot and the flaming torch in Genesis 15:17, each representing God, pass through the pieces, symbolizing God's commitment to the covenant for both himself and Abram. As Christians, we see a hint of God's promise that will be fulfilled in Jesus on the cross, declaring truly, "It is finished" (John 19:30).

In the midst of this amazing promise, God warns Abram that a time is coming when his descendants will be enslaved for four hundred years in a foreign land (Gen. 15:13–14). When God and Abram cut this deal, Abram is living in Canaan with his family. So how is it that his descendants end up living in a foreign nation far from home, strangers in a land not theirs? The final chapters of Genesis answer this question.

With severe drought and famine in Canaan, Jacob (who is Abram's grandson) and his sons seek food in the breadbasket of Egypt along the perennial Nile River (Gen. 42:1–5).

The Nile provided water throughout the year, making it possible to grow and irrigate crops along the banks as well as offering tremendous wealth for the Egyptians through trade and water transport.

Evergreen fields along the Nile River

Under the "serendipitous" leadership of Joseph (Jacob's second youngest son), Jacob's family makes a home in Egypt. Genesis draws to a close with Joseph's full confidence in God's faithfulness to "surely come to your aid and take you [Jacob's descendants] up out of this land to the land he promised" (Gen. 50:24).

The descendants of Jacob—called the Israelites or Hebrews—become successful in Egypt and also exceedingly numerous in obedience to God's first command to "be fruitful and increase in number" (Gen. 1:28; Ex 1:7). Israel's miraculous fertility, even in exile, is a fulfillment of God's promise to Abraham to make him into "a great nation" (Gen. 12:2); and, as we will see later in the story, this stands in defiant victory against Pharaoh's attempts to control and kill their population.

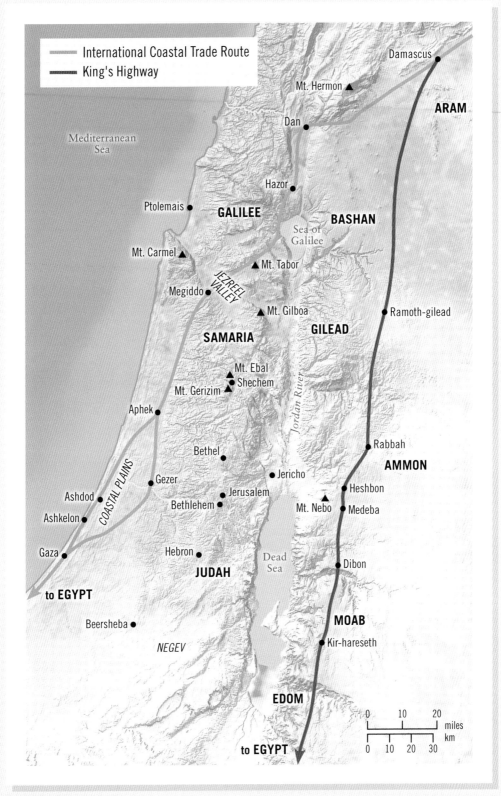

International Coastal Trade Route
King's Highway

Damascus

Mt. Hermon ▲

ARAM

Dan

Mediterranean
Sea

Hazor

Ptolemais

GALILEE

BASHAN

Sea of
Galilee

Mt. Carmel ▲

JEZREEL VALLEY

▲ Mt. Tabor

Megiddo

▲ Mt. Gilboa

GILEAD

SAMARIA

Ramoth-gilead

Mt. Ebal ▲
Shechem

Mt. Gerizim ▲

Jordan River

Aphek

Bethel

Rabbah

AMMON

Gezer

Jericho

Jerusalem

Heshbon

Ashdod

COASTAL PLAINS

Bethlehem

Mt. Nebo ▲

Medeba

Ashkelon

Gaza

Hebron

Dead
Sea

Dibon

to EGYPT

JUDAH

Beersheba ●

MOAB

NEGEV

Kir-hareseth

EDOM

0   10   20
miles
km
0   10   20   30

to EGYPT

A New King of Egypt

The success of the Israelites does not sit well with the new king of Egypt, who does not remember Joseph's faithfulness to the empire. No matter the label outsiders are given—stranger, immigrant, foreigner, alien—newcomers are always met with fear and suspicion. Fearing the growing population of Israelites, the new pharaoh brutally enslaves them through forced labor and ruthless oppression. Miraculously, the more the Israelites are oppressed, the more they increase.

The Egyptian Empire

While the Bible does not name the pharaoh of the exodus, Ramses II is a possible contender. His reign corresponded with the rise of the Hyksos, an Egyptian term referring to a large group of Semitic immigrants from the coastal and inland areas of Canaan. The Hyksos settled in the eastern Delta of the Nile River and gradually took political control in Lower Egypt and ruled it until their expulsion in the latter half of the sixteenth century BC. The Egyptians resolved that such a foreign threat should never be allowed to take hold within their kingdom again. They shored up their defenses, investing in garrisons and military might, ultimately defending the northern entrance into Egypt by expanding north into the region of Canaan, controlling the International Coastal Trade Route as well as the King's Highway.

Ramses II

In Egypt, it was customary for a new king to free those enslaved and imprisoned under the previous regime. The Egyptian hymn "Joy at the Accession of Ramses IV," written when Ramses IV became pharaoh (c. 1164–1157 BC), declares, "They who were in prison are set free; they who were fettered are in joy." The hymn goes on to describe the custom of granting amnesty to those persecuted under the previous regime: "They that had fled have come (back) to their towns, and they that were hidden have come forth (again)."* (This custom perhaps explains why, later in the exodus story, Moses is able to return to Egypt; Ex. 4:19.) Unfortunately, the new king in the exodus story does not celebrate with freedom, but doubles down on oppression, making labor harder and brutality greater. We can understand why the Israelites cried out so desperately to God when the new pharaoh provided no mercy.

The God Who Takes Notice

In Exodus 2:23–25, God responds to the Israelites' four outcries with four corresponding actions:

ISRAELITES	GOD
• Groaned (v. 23)	• Heard (v. 24)
• Cried out (v. 23)	• Remembered (v. 24)
• Cried for help (v. 23)	• Looked upon (v. 25)
• Moaned (or groaned, v. 24)	• Took notice (concerned, v. 25)

What causes God to act on behalf of Israel? Did their righteousness provoke his compassion? Did the Israelites use the correct words when praying or address God in just the right way? (Later, we'll

---

* Translation of the Egyptian Hymn taken from *Ancient Near Eastern Texts Relating to the Old Testament* edited by James B. Pritchard (Princeton University Press).

see that Moses does not even know God's name and must ask for it at the burning bush!) God simply hears their cries. We have a God who hears. Our God cares when people—all people—cry out. The Lord does not allow the cries of the sufferers, no matter who they are or who they do or do not worship, to echo into nothingness. God takes note. God cares. God hears, even when no one else does.

God *remembers*. We might be taken aback when we read "God remembered," as though God has forgotten all about his people and thinks, "Oh, right! The Israelites. I know those people!" The Hebrew word *zahar*, "remember," means much more than a simple, passive, mental recall exercise; it means to be mindful, to think upon, and then act. In fact, the exodus narrative is characterized by echoes of divine promise. From generation to generation, from Abraham to Moses, God is remembering his promise to "take note" of Israel. In Genesis, as Joseph speaks a final address to his brothers, he says, "I am about to die. But God will surely come to your aid [Hebrew: *p-k-d* "take notice of you"] and take you up out of this land to the land he promised on oath to Abraham, Isaac and Jacob" (Gen. 50:24).

This promise, that God would "take note" (*p-k-d*) was handed down from generation to generation. The same phrase is used when the Lord "was gracious" to Sarah and gives her Isaac (Gen. 21:1); when Naomi hears that the Lord has come to the aid of his people (Ruth 1:6); when God takes note of Hannah and gives her a son (1 Sam. 1:19–20); and when Israel is exiled in Babylon and God reminds them that he has a plan to prosper them and not to harm them (Jer. 29:10–11). The Hebrew root *p-k-d* powerfully communicates the direct involvement and intervention of God in human affairs.

When God appears to Moses at the burning bush, God reminds Moses of this promise, declaring, "Go, assemble the elders of Israel and say to them, 'The LORD, the God of your fathers—the God of Abraham, Isaac and Jacob—appeared to me and said: I have *watched over you and have seen* [*p-k-d, p-k-d*] what has been done to you in Egypt" (Ex. 3:16). God has taken note. The doubling of this root adds strong emphasis to the divine faithfulness. This Hebrew root is repeated throughout Exodus (Ex. 3:16; 4:31; 13:19; 20:5; 32:34). When God takes note, we can be confident of a divine visitation and intervention in our lives. God is not simply remembering that a people Israel exist, God is acting to fulfill the evergreen covenantal promises of long ago.

When God hears and remembers, God then acts: "I have *heard* the groaning of the Israelites, whom the Egyptians are enslaving, and I have *remembered* my covenant" (Ex. 6:5). Therefore, God "will free … deliver … redeem … [and] take you as my own people" (Ex. 6:6–7 NRSVUE). Israel's four outcries bring about four divine responses, which in turn, bring about God's four miraculous acts. These four acts are memorialized today in the retelling of the exodus at Passover Seders around the world every spring, as four cups of wine are served, each cup representing God's four acts.

	ISRAEL'S OUTCRY Ex. 2:23-25	GOD'S RESPONSE Ex. 6:5	MIRACULOUS ACTS Ex. 6:6-7
1	Groaned	Heard	Freedom (bring you out)
2	Cried out	Remembered	Deliverance (deliver you)
3	Cried for help	Looked upon	Redemption (redeem you)
4	Moaned/groaned	Took notice	Betrothal (take you)

God is not faithless. God is not absent. God is not hard-hearted. God cares about our suffering. God cares about injustice and oppression, and he will do something about it.

For four hundred years the Israelites suffered oppression and injustice. No doubt, many during those long years wondered if God would ever be faithful to his covenantal promises to Abraham. Like many in this world, they never experienced freedom, deliverance, or justice in their lifetimes. Does this mean that God is unfaithful? No, for we are living in a God-centric story. God is faithful, even if we are not personally receiving deliverance on this side of heaven.

Martin Luther King, Jr., noted, "The arc of the moral universe is long, but it bends toward justice." If we never see freedom or justice in our own lives, we cannot give up. God is faithful. As we wait for deliverance, may we seek out ways to partner with God and tug on that arc to bend it toward the justice God is calling us to—on earth as it is in heaven.

Upon hearing the cries of Israel, God hears, remembers, looks upon, and takes notice. When we or our loved ones are in the midst of difficult times, may we follow God's example and take time to listen to the suffering and remind ourselves of God's faithful promises to act.

Life Application Questions

1. When in your life have you felt truly *heard* by God?

2. Think of a time when you heard a cry of injustice, a cry so deep and piercing that you simply had to act. What was the situation and what did you do?

3. Do you feel the weight of oppression in an area of your life right now? What is your prayer—your crying out—to God?

4. If you don't see God's rescue as soon as you would like, what are some ways you can deal with the disappointment?

5. Do you know a person or people crying out in suffering right now? How might God be calling you to help bring about relief and rescue?

Notes

Notes

2
GOD ACTS

Moses Drawn from
the Nile River

God Acts

Like an expert weaver, the writer of Exodus interlaces vibrant and diverse colors to create a beautiful tapestry. In the narrative, threads of divine actions weave in and out alongside seemingly mundane human undertakings. The deceptively simple story of the child Moses is no exception.

As we'll see in this session, the story of the exodus can be understood as a retelling of the creation account from the book of Genesis. Ever since humanity's exile from the garden of Eden, God has sought ways to re-create the world and set it right again.

In this next part of the exodus story, there may not be any great seas parting, no staffs turning into snakes, or swarms of locusts filling the sky, but God's power is certainly not absent. He is active. He creates and preserves life—and the miracle is that we get to be part of his good plan.

Read It

Key Bible Passage

For this session, read Exodus 1:15–2:25.

Optional Reading

Genesis 1:1–2:3; 6:9–22

"She got a papyrus basket for him and coated it with tar and pitch. Then she placed the child in it and put it among the reeds along the bank of the Nile."

EXODUS 2:3

Know It

1. Who are the characters (named and unnamed) in this Bible passage?

2. The characters in this passage take many risks. What do each of these risk-takers have to lose by their actions? What do you think motivates each of them?

3. Which character do you identify with the most? Why?

The Disobedient Midwives

In an attempt to control the population and power of the Hebrews (the Israelites), the king of Egypt tells the Hebrew midwives that all Hebrew boys must be killed at birth. But the midwives, named Shiphrah and Puah, fearing God, participate in the first recorded act of civil disobedience in the Bible—and amongst the earliest in recorded history. These women disobey Pharaoh's directive, preserving the lives of the Hebrew boys. When questioned, they lie to Pharaoh, saying that Hebrew women are so vigorous that they give birth before a midwife has the chance to arrive. (The subtext being that Hebrew women cannot help but bring forth life!)

Pharaoh and the Midwives

Shiphrah, a Semitic name, means "beautiful." Puah, a Ugaritic name, originally meant "blossom" and later came to mean "girl." These women not only disobey the murderous king, but they put their own lives at risk in order to bring forth life in the world. It's no wonder the Bible preserves the esteemed names of these courageous women, while the all-powerful Pharaoh remains unnamed.

Pharaoh becomes so enraged at the continuing success and growth of the Hebrews that he orders his people to throw every newborn Hebrew boy into the Nile River. It is against the backdrop of this murderous decree that a couple named Amram and Jochebed (both from the tribe of Levi) have a son who will be called Moses.

A New Beginning

When Jochebed gives birth to Moses, she hides him for three months in defiance of Pharaoh's murderous decree. She sees that her son is *ki-tov*, often translated in Exodus 2:2 as "fine," "good," "healthy," or "beautiful." In Genesis 1, this same phrase, *ki-tov*, is repeated seven times by God when he looks upon his creation (verses 4, 10, 12, 18, 21, 25, 31). With the birth of Moses, a new creation is breaking in to human history, and once again, this creation enters the world hovering over waters of chaos, calling forth order and life. Jochebed sees it and knows that it is *good*.

No longer able to hide her son in her own home, Moses's mother ingeniously "complies" with Pharaoh's decree and hides her child in plain sight. She gently places Moses in a papyrus basket, coated with tar and pitch, and strategically sets him amongst the reeds along the bank of the Nile River where she knows Pharaoh's daughter bathes.

Pharaoh's daughter finding baby Moses

The Hebrew word for the papyrus basket is *tevah*, and it occurs only one other place in the Bible: in Genesis 6:14 to describe Noah's ark. That's right; the same word is used for both a baby basket and a giant floating zoo! As Jesus teaches us, every jot and tittle in the Bible matters (Matt. 5:18). So why does Scripture use the word *tevah* specifically? When faced with wickedness and a need for deliverance, only a *tevah* will do. In Moses's time, just like in Noah's time, wickedness is rampant. The world needs a re-creation. Thus, this redeeming vessel comes upon the scene to bring deliverance anew. Pharaoh tried to make the Nile waters

Papyrus basket

a source of death for the Hebrew boys, but for Moses (and all Israel for that matter), God's instrument of deliverance and life is drawn up out of the waters by none other than the daughter of Pharaoh. Just as Noah and his family were saved from the flood waters, so, too, Moses and his family will be delivered from the watery grave of the Nile.

Pharaoh's daughter takes pity on the child she finds, saying, "This is one of the Hebrew babies" (Ex. 2:6). She knows of her father's

Moses's Parents

Though unnamed in Exodus 2, Moses's parents' names are recorded in Exodus 6:20: Amram and Jochebed. Amram's name means "mighty nation" and Jochebed's name declares "the Lord is glory," foreshadowing Israel's destiny. In the Old Testament, names often carry destinies for the individuals or indicate what will come to pass in the biblical story.

decree, yet she, like the midwives, also chooses civil disobedience to save a life. And not just any life, but she rescues the life of the one who will deliver God's people from Egypt.

From a distance, Moses's sister Miriam watches the scene unfold. One can only imagine the fear Miriam must have felt for her brother and their family during the months of hiding his existence and then the risky plan to save his life. This young Hebrew slave orchestrates, not only a reunion for her mother and brother, but also payment for Jochebed to nurse her own son. Moses is returned to the aching arms of his mother and there he remains, thriving under her loving physical, emotional, and spiritual care. When he is old enough to join Pharaoh's household, the princess takes him as her own, raising him as an Egyptian son. She names him Moses, a common Egyptian name meaning "to be born,

Moses's Sister

Miriam's name means both "bitter" and "rebellious." Perhaps she felt the intensity of bitter injustice and pain, and yearned to rebel against the empire and its powers. It is no wonder her name, and its Greek equivalent *Mary*, became one of the most popular female names, with at least six different women named Mary in the New Testament. Jesus's own mother lives up to this name when she sings her own rebellious song against oppressors (Luke 1:46–55).

Miriam and Jochebed

a child, a son." The author of Exodus connects the name to a Hebrew root, *m-sh-h*, which can also mean "to draw up/out of water," as the Egyptian princess declares, "because I drew him out of the water" (Ex. 2:10).

Present realities and future hopes weave through our biblical text, for just as Moses is drawn out of the water, Moses will be God's instrument to draw Israel out of the waters of the sea, from death to life (Ex. 14:21; Isa. 63:11).

A Stranger in a Strange Land

Time passes and Moses grows up. As we are introduced to Moses the adult, we see that his two identities are both present within him. Following the example of his Egyptian mother who *saw* the basket among the reeds and *saw* it was a child, Moses *saw* the burdens of the Hebrews. He *saw* the violent beating of "one of his own people," identifying with his Hebrew family (Ex. 2:11). He *saw* that no one was about and struck the Egyptian beating the Hebrew slave. Righteous anger is a complex emotion, and, in this case, Moses imitates the brutal behavior of the taskmaster, ultimately killing him.

When Moses's crime becomes known, Pharaoh tries to kill him, so Moses leaves every home he has ever known and flees to the desert of Midian. Moses, the "Egyptian" (Ex. 2:19), settles in Midian. He embraces his new life in the desert, becoming a shepherd and marrying Zipporah, who is a daughter of a priest of Midian.

When Zipporah gives birth to a son, Moses names him Gershom, because "I have become a stranger in a strange land" (Ex. 2:22). The Hebrew word *ger* means "stranger" or "foreigner" and *shom* means "there," recalling God's promise to Abraham: "Your descendants will be strangers in a country not their own" (Gen. 15:13). God has not forgotten. God is at work, even as he seems far off. Every moment of the exodus story is divinely orchestrated by a God not seen.

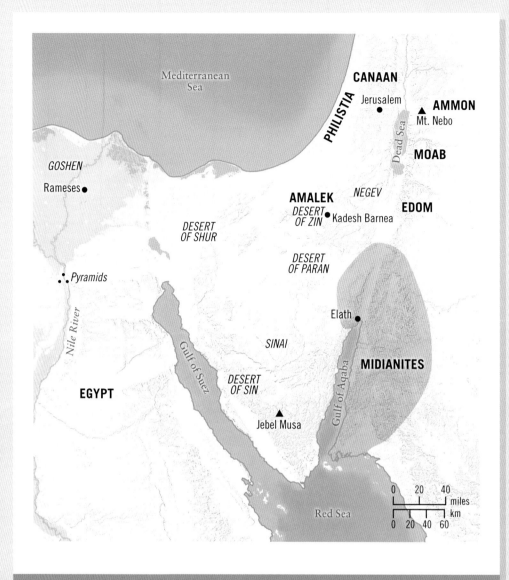

The Midianites

Genesis indicates that the Midianites were descendants of Abraham (Gen. 25:1–2). They were a nomadic desert people who lived in the wilderness that stretched from the Gulf of Aqaba up through the Syrian-Arabian Desert, and into the southern borders of what would become Israel, living just west and northwest of Elath.

Live It

Many of us strive to be the best in our field, have the most followers on social media, or earn the most awards, achievements, and accolades. Likewise, major heroic figures like Noah, Abraham, and Moses feature prominently in our sermons and Bible studies, and we seek to follow in their footsteps. Yet the deliverance of Israel in the exodus story hinges entirely on the courage and faithfulness of a few "minor" characters. Without the disobedience of the midwives, the bravery of Jochebed, and the rebelliousness of Miriam and of Pharaoh's own daughter, the deliverance of God's people from Egypt would never have happened.

Perhaps one reason Moses becomes so compassionate toward the marginalized is because his life was shaped by strong, intuitive women who acted on behalf of the oppressed themselves. Moses does not become Moses without a community of courageous women. May we never doubt the significance of our role in God's great story. God is at work in each of us, whether we are billed as major or minor characters in the story. He partners with anyone who is willing to follow him and be obedient to his word. The long arc bends toward justice through a faithful partnership between God and those who take hold and pull.

Life Application Questions

1. Maybe you've heard the story of "baby Moses in the basket" many times before—in movies, art, or storybooks. What stood out to you this time, when reading the account solely from the words of Scripture?

2. Where do you see God moving in this part of the exodus story?

3. The midwives disobey Pharaoh's order and lie to him. Describe a situation where lying and disobeying an order would actually be the best thing to do.

4. When have you taken a risk to right an injustice or to help rescue someone? What motivated you to act?

5. Maybe you've thought, "I could never be a Moses or an Abraham!" Does reflecting on the importance of "minor" characters in the story change how you see your role in God's work?

3
GOD RESCUES

The Burning Bush

God Rescues

At this point in the exodus narrative, it has been some time since the Israelites first cried out. Four hundred years of slavery to be precise. It's been a lifetime since a baby was placed in a basket and rescued by Pharaoh's daughter. Suffering, pain, and evil continue to be the daily companions of enslaved Israel.

When and how will God finally rescue his people?

How would *we* do it? Maybe raise awareness through wealthy donors and popular influencers? Hold fundraisers? Find a charismatic and enthusiastic person to lead the charge?

God took a different approach.

Step one: commission an eighty-year-old shepherd hiding in exile who doesn't even want to go!

Read It

Key Bible Passage

For this session, read Exodus 3:1–4:18.

Optional Reading

Exodus 4:19–7:13

"Take off your sandals, for the place where you are standing is holy ground."

EXODUS 3:5

Know It

1. What are God's first words to Moses? What are Moses's first words to God?

2. What are Moses's five objections (questions and pleas) to God's calling and God's response to each objection?

	MOSES'S OBJECTION	GOD'S RESPONSE
1		
2		
3		
4		
5		

"Here I am"

No longer an Egyptian prince, Moses has made a new life for himself as a shepherd, tending flocks in the desert just like his ancestors. (According to the book of Acts, Moses spent forty years in Midian; Acts 7:23–30.) Then, in the middle of an ordinary desert, on a day like any other, God shows up a burning bush.

Moses sees that a bush is on fire but not consumed, and the phenomenon piques his curiosity. He must stop and watch this bush. (Just like the Israelites suffering in Egypt, the bush is on fire but not consumed.) Once God sees that Moses has turned to watch, God calls out, "Moses! Moses!" Moses responds, "*Hineni,*" which means "Here I am." This simple response is anything but simplistic. It declares a full presence, awareness, and openness to the call of God. Moses echoes the faithful responses of his ancestors Abraham and Jacob (Gen. 22:1; 31:11). Future Israelites like Samuel and Mary will follow their examples as well, hearing God's call and declaring, "Here I am" (1 Sam. 3:4; Luke 1:38).

Fire in the Bible

Formless, powerful, bringing warmth and light—fire often signifies the presence of God in the Bible, and this is especially so in the exodus story: God spoke to Moses from a burning bush (Ex. 3:2); a pillar of fire guided the Israelites' journey after they left Egypt (Ex. 13:21); God descended upon Mount Sinai in fire (Ex. 19:18); he made his presence known through a cloud that resembled fire resting upon the tabernacle (Num. 9:15–16).

God says to Moses, "Do not come any closer.... Take off your sandals, for the place where you are standing is holy ground.... I am the God of your father, the God of Abraham, the God of Isaac, and the God of Jacob" (Ex. 3:5–6).

Afraid to look at God, Moses hides his face, and as is traditional in the ancient Near East, he removes his shoes, a sign of humility and respect for divine presence. This practice continued throughout biblical times (see Josh. 5:15). When priestly clothing is described in the Bible, shoes are not mentioned because they were not worn during service in the tabernacle or temple. In many synagogues today, Jews who trace their ancestry through the priestly line of Aaron remove their shoes before pronouncing over the people the blessing found in Numbers 6:22–27.

A Land of Milk and Honey

Once God has Moses's attention, he declares:

> I have indeed seen the misery of my people in Egypt. I have heard them crying out because of their slave drivers, and I am concerned about their suffering. So I have come down to rescue them from the hand of the Egyptians and to bring them up out of that land into a good and spacious land, a land flowing with milk and honey. (Ex. 3:7–8)

Reaching back into the past to grab hold of ancient covenants and looking toward the future, God reiterates his promise of a land "flowing with milk and honey." Coming from the lush Nile delta in Egypt where one could just irrigate crops "by foot" (Deut. 11:10), it was necessary to remind the Israelites of the beautiful land God will provide. While their new land would have the Jordan River, it could not compare to mighty rivers like the Nile, Tigris, or Euphrates found in other ancient empires. Instead, the promised land's strength lied in its diversity. From the snowcapped mountains of Hermon in the north to the rich alluvial soil well suited for growing fruit trees, wheat, and barley in Galilee, from

the broad coastal plains leading up through valleys to the terraced
Judean hillsides, and then to the Negev desert in the south—
Israel has the same regional diversity as California within an area
smaller than New Jersey.

▲ Mt. Hermon

GALILEE

Sea of
Galilee

Mt. Carmel ▲

Mediterranean
Sea

▲ Mt. Tabor

JEZREEL
VALLEY

▲ Mt. Gilboa

SAMARIA

▲ Mt. Ebal
▲ Mt. Gerizim

Jordan River

Jerusalem ●

COASTAL PLAINS

JUDEA

▲ Mt. Nebo

Dead
Sea

0   10   20
                miles
              km
0   10   20   30

NEGEV

"Milk and honey" sounds odd (and sticky!) to our modern ears, but to the ancient Israelites, this description indicates the fertility and desirability of the land.

- Milk in the ancient Near East was provided mainly by goats and sheep. Milk indicates a land good for shepherding, providing dairy products, meat, hides, and hair and fleece for clothing and tents.

- Honey in the Bible most often refers to the thick syrup made from dates. Honey indicates an agricultural land, good for crops and fruit trees.

A land of milk and honey is a land diverse enough and large enough for both nomadic shepherds and settled farmers to live in harmony. In other words, it is a land that can sustain all of Abraham's descendants.

Date honey

Moses's Questions

Understandably, Moses has many questions and concerns about returning to Egypt where there is a warrant out for his life. He engages in an incredible dialogue with the Creator of the universe, starting with the question, "Who am I that I should go to Pharaoh and bring the Israelites out of Egypt?" (Ex. 3:11).

Fair question. Moses could pass for an Egyptian decades ago when he arrived in Midian, but he is no longer a resident of opulent palaces. He is now a tent dweller. With sheep and goats as his daily companions, he is anathema to the Egyptians (Gen. 46:34). But he is the right choice. Moses has demonstrated an intolerance for injustice, he is knowledgeable about the Egyptian power structure, and he has decades of practice shepherding a stubborn flock. His humility makes him the ideal leader for God's people— and that stands in stark contrast to the arrogance of Pharaoh, who will, later in the story, not ask, "Who am I?" but instead scoff, "Who is the LORD?" (Ex. 5:2).

When Moses asks God, "Who am I that I should go to Pharaoh?" God does not prop Moses up with compliments or assurances, describing the heroic qualities of the human before him. God simply says, "I will be [*ehyeh*] with you" (Ex. 3:12). Moses is not the hero of the story. Yet God is not asking Moses to go to Pharaoh alone. God, the Creator of the universe—the God of Abraham, Isaac, and Jacob—will be with Moses as he stands before Pharaoh.

Since the garden of Eden, we have a God who not only is *willing* to be with us but also *longs* to be with us, walking in the cool of the day (Gen. 3:8). God promises to be with Moses. God promises to be with us. Generations later, Jesus, the Immanuel—"God with us" (Isa. 7:14; Matt. 1:23)—will arrive. He will choose twelve disciples to be with him (Mark 3:14). And when sending the disciples out to the powers and nations of their own day, he will promise, "I am with you always" (Matt. 28:20). The calling may be daunting, even seem impossible, but we are not alone.

Not surprisingly, Moses has a few more questions: "If the Israelites ask me, 'What is his name?' What shall I tell them?" God responds:

> I AM WHO I AM.... You shall say to the Israelites: "I AM has sent me to you.... The LORD, the God of your ancestors, the God of Abraham, the God of Isaac, and the God of Jacob, has sent me to you." This is my name forever, and this my title for all generations. (Ex. 3:14–15 NRSVUE)

Throughout the biblical narrative, great emphasis is placed on the power and destiny of names. With the exception of Sarah's Egyptian slave Hagar who names God *El-Roi* ("God who sees me"; Gen. 16:13), God is the one who gives names—and often changes them: Abram to Abraham, Sarai to Sarah, and Jacob to Israel. In the ancient Near East, to name someone was to define them or have authority over that person, like a parent naming a child. Name giving implied the wielding of power over the one named; hence, the divine name can only proceed from God him. Moses may know the name of God, but God's name of himself, by definition, indicates that Moses (or anyone) cannot control or define God.

God says he is "*ehyeh-asher-ehyeh*," "I AM WHO I AM." Another translation could be "I will be who I will be." The precise ancient pronunciation is lost to us today, but its meaning is not. The very utterance of the words in Hebrew sounds like breath flowing in and out of our lungs. Just as God breathed into humans, giving them life (Gen. 2:7), God is breathing new life into his oppressed people. The Lord, ruler of all life, will be who he will be.

Snakes

One of the signs God gave Moses was Moses's staff turning into a snake, and then back again into a staff. Staffs and snakes had powerful resonances in ancient Egypt. The staff was a symbol of royal authority and power, held in the hands of many an Egyptian king. The menacing snake, worn over the headdresses of the kings, represented the Egyptian cobra goddess, Uraeus, and reinforced the connection between Pharaoh and the gods. Later in the exodus story when Moses and Aaron stand before Pharaoh, the snakes of Pharaoh's magicians are devoured by Aaron's snake, demonstrating the Lord's supremacy over all others (Ex. 7:8–12).

That settled, Moses continues his protests: "What if they do not believe me or listen to me?" (Ex. 4:1). God compassionately and patiently engages with Moses's what-ifs, providing answers, signs, and wonders that will persuade the Israelites, as well as the Egyptians, of God's sovereignty.

Moses's final objection to God's call is "I'm a terrible speaker!" But when that doesn't change God's mind, he pleads, "Send someone else!" (Ex. 4:10, 13). With patience exhausted, and a brief lecture about God being the Creator of mouths, God ultimately agrees to send along Aaron, Moses's brother, to join the mission.

With all his objections addressed, Moses accepts God's calling to be part of a divine rescue plan and to return to the place of his birth, the place he fled for his life years earlier.

Live It

In Genesis 28, Jacob, the grandson of Abraham, rests for a night while on a long journey that will take him far from home. While Jacob is asleep on the ground, God sends him a dream of a stairway filled with angels reaching from earth to heaven. In this vision, God promises to bless Jacob and be with him always. When Jacob wakes up, he exclaims, "Surely the LORD is in this place—and I did not know it!" (Gen. 28:16 NRSVUE). Like Jacob, Moses also is unaware of a divine presence in the desert—that is, until God speaks to him from a bush.

Elizabeth Barrett Browning observed, "Earth is crammed with heaven, and every common bush afire with God; but only he who sees takes off his shoes." May we be people who anticipate encounters with God's presence in this world. May we be among the first to kick off our sandals and roll up our proverbial sleeves, partnering with God in bringing rescue to the world.

Life Application Questions

1. What does the divine name "I am who I am" (or "I will be who I will be") tell you about God?

2. Have you ever been in a situation where you could say, "God is here, and I didn't know it!"? Share or journal about that experience.

3. Have you ever sought God for a sign to confirm something he might have been telling you? Is there something you need confirmation about in your life now?

4. Read Exodus 4:29–31. God came through for Moses, just as he said he would. How much confidence do you have that God will come through for you?

5. How might God be calling you to be part of his rescue plan to set captives free and to unburden the oppressed? How will you respond to God's call?

Notes

Notes

GOD REIGNS

*Ten Plagues and
the Crossing of the Sea*

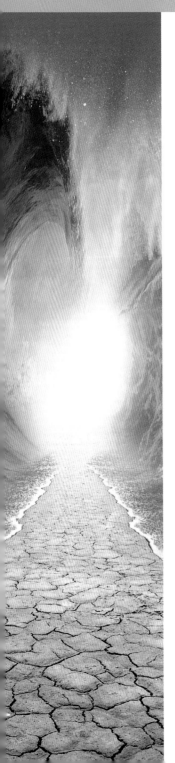

God Reigns

Rescue takes time, it is never easy, and things often get worse before they get better. Before Moses set out to return to Egypt, God warned him that Pharaoh's heart would be hard, and deliverance would only happen by God's mighty hand. Sure enough, when Moses and Aaron first confront Pharaoh, requesting the release of the Hebrew slaves, not only is their request rejected, but also Pharaoh's cruelty intensifies, increasing his slaves' workload. The people are angry, and Moses laments to God, "Why, Lord, why have you brought trouble on this people? Is this why you sent me?... You have not rescued your people at all" (Ex. 5:22–23). Fear, hardship, despair, and doubt are unavoidable companions when we are engaged in the work of justice. Evil does not take kindly to confrontation.

We'll see in this session how God sends ten terrifying demonstrations of his sovereignty and wonder, ten chances for Pharaoh to do the right thing—but Pharaoh's heart is hard. Egypt is tossed into chaos, from the Nile River to the fields, proving that Pharaoh is powerless against the true Lord, the God who reigns above all false gods.

Read It

Key Bible Passage

For this session, read Exodus 12:21–42 and 14:5–31.

Optional Reading

Exodus 7:14–15:21

"Moses stretched out his hand over the sea, and all that night the LORD drove the sea back with a strong east wind and turned it into dry land."

EXODUS 14:21

1. The best stories are full of unexpected twists and turns. What happened in the exodus narrative that was probably unexpected by the people living the story?

2. What happened that finally changed Pharaoh's mind (or heart), and what changed it back?

3. The Israelites also wavered. In what ways did they change in the face of different circumstances?

Pharaoh's Hard Heart

The hardening of Pharaoh's heart appears twenty times in the exodus narrative. Ten times, it is Pharaoh himself who hardens his heart (Ex. 7:13, 14, 22; 8:11, 15, 28; 9:7, 34, 35; 13:15), and in the other ten times, God causes Pharaoh's heart to be hard (Ex. 4:21; 7:3; 9:12; 10:1, 20, 27; 11:10; 14:4, 8, 17). God hardening Pharaoh's heart was God giving the king of Egypt over to his own inclination toward evil, allowing his obstinance to become his destiny. Why does God do this? So that everyone will know there is no one like the Lord in all the earth:

> Then the LORD said to Moses, "Get up early in the morning, confront Pharaoh and say to him, 'This is what the LORD, the God of the Hebrews, says: Let my people go, so that they may worship me, or this time I will send the full force of my plagues against you and against your officials and your people, *so you may know that there is no one like me in all the earth.* For by now I could have stretched out my hand and struck you and your people with a plague that would have wiped you off the earth. *But I have raised you up for this very purpose, that I might show you my power and that my name might be proclaimed in all the earth.* (Ex. 9:13–16)

Each of the ten plagues serve as a commentary on the powerlessness of Pharaoh and the Egyptian gods in the face of the one true Lord of Israel. In the exodus, both the Israelites and the Egyptians come to understand there is only one true God reigning over all creation—and he is not Pharaoh.

The Ten Plagues

Measure for measure, God calls the oppressors to account and sees that justice is done. Consider the first plague in which the Nile River turns to blood. Pharaoh had decreed the killing of all Hebrew baby boys by casting them into the Nile. Like Abel's blood which called out to God from the ground (Gen. 2), God had not forgotten the lives lost in Egypt, nor did God allow the perpetrators to forget.

Exodus 12:12 states that God's judgment came upon "all the gods of Egypt" (see also Num. 33:4). Archaeologists are uncertain which particular deities were being worshiped in Egypt during the time of the exodus. Much of the information about Egyptian gods actually comes from a different location and time period in Egyptian history. Despite this uncertainty, it is still beneficial to consider possible connections between the plagues and Egyptian deities to see how each plague directly proved the Lord's superiority over powerless and false gods.

The Heavy Heart

The concept of a hard, or heavy, heart was well known in Egypt. After death, the Egyptians believed that *Ma'at*, the Egyptian goddess of truth and justice, weighed the

heart of the deceased against a feather. If one's heart was lighter than a feather, then the person's deeds were righteous, but if the heart was heavy, then judgment was meted out in the afterlife.

The Weighing of the Heart ritual

1. Blood

- The Nile River was turned into blood. The Nile was the primary source for fresh water, supporting life through irrigation, trade, and transportation. Pharaoh had turned it into a place of death when he commanded the Hebrew baby boys be drowned in its waters.

Khnum

- *Hapi*, the god of the annual flooding of the Nile, was worshiped and given offerings. The flooding itself was believed to be a manifestation of the god *Osiris*. *Khnum* was the god of the source of the Nile.

- Pharaoh's magicians could not reverse the plague of blood, but only duplicate it.

2. Frogs

- As frogs fled the bloody Nile, they invaded the land, eventually dying and creating a terrible stench throughout the land.

- The goddess *Heqet* was represented by a frog. She was the consort of the god *Khnum* and was considered to be the goddess of fertility, assisting women in childbirth. This plague may have been considered retribution for the decree ordering the midwives to kill Hebrew newborns.

- Pharaoh's magicians could not reverse the plague but only create more frogs. This plague caused Pharaoh to beg for mercy and acknowledge the existence of the Lord for the first time. But he soon hardened his heart again.

3. Gnats

- Dust turned into small gnat-like insects, possibly lice.

- *Geb* was the Egyptian god of the earth, and gnats come from the dust of the earth.

- The magicians could neither ease nor duplicate this plague, causing them to declare, "This is the finger of God" (Ex. 8:19). (Jesus echoes this phrase in Luke 11:20: "But if I drive out demons by the finger of God, then the kingdom of God has come upon you.") The magicians realized that the rule and reign of God was upon them.

4. Flies

- The Hebrew word for these insects (*'arov*) is unclear, as the word only occurs here in Exodus. These insects might have been something like flies or mosquitoes. Psalm 78:45 says they "devoured" (or "fed on") the Egyptians.

Fresco of Khepri in the Tomb of Queen Nefertari

- *Khepri* was the god with a fly or scarab beetle for a head. If the Egyptians considered the source of the plague to be *Khepri*, then why did the plague of flies not also affect those in Goshen where the Hebrew slaves lived? Answer: The source of this plague could only be God alone.

- For the first time in the plagues, a clear distinction was made between the Egyptians and the Israelites (Ex. 8:22–23).

5. Death of Livestock

- A plague was sent on the Egyptians' livestock in the fields, but the Israelites' livestock remained unharmed.

- *Hathor* was the mother and sky goddess, represented by a cow. *Apis* was pictured as a bull sacrificed and reborn.

- While the third plague was seen as having come from the "finger of God" (Ex. 8:19), this fifth plague was from the "hand of the LORD" (Ex. 9:3). No mistake could be made as to the source of the plague.

6. Boils

- In front of Pharaoh, Moses tossed handfuls of soot into the air, which caused festering boils to appear on both the Egyptians and their animals.

- *Imhotep* was the god of healing and medicine. *Sekmet* was the goddess of healing.

- The magicians were also afflicted with boils and could do nothing to help.

7. Hail

- A massive hailstorm struck people, animals, and crops, but did not fall in Goshen where the Israelites lived. God warned the Egyptian officials to seek shelter, but only some took heed.

- *Set* was the Egyptian god of storms and disorder. *Nut* was the goddess of the sky.

- This plague showed that "the earth is the LORD's" (Ex. 9:29) and that God alone was sovereign over all of creation.

8. Locusts

- Egyptian officials begged Pharaoh to let the people go, but he did not listen. So locusts destroyed every plant not lost in the hailstorm. (A locust swarm can devour as much as 100,000 tons of vegetation in single night!)

- *Serapia* was the god with the head of a locust who protected against locusts—clearly powerless in this plague!

9. Darkness

- Intense darkness, possibly caused by a dense sandstorm, fell upon the land for three days, blotting out the sun. This darkness could be "felt" or "touched" (Ex. 10:21), likely referring to the particles of sand and dust in the air. The darkness lasted three days, corresponding to the three-day journey Pharaoh would not permit the Israelites to travel into the wilderness to worship their God. The land of Goshen, however, was spared from the darkness.

- *Ra, Amon-ra, Atum,* and *Horus* were gods associated with the sun. For Egyptians, the sun-god was the supreme god, worshiped in the palace ritual. Pharaoh himself was said to be the earthly representative of this god.

- This plague demonstrated that even the most powerful Egyptian god was no god at all.

10. Death of the Firstborn

- The last and final plague struck dead firstborn males, including Pharaoh's son, but the spirit of death passed over homes with blood of a lamb on their doorframes, sparing the lives of all those inside.

- This plague was an attack on the lineage and deity of Pharaoh himself: "This is what the LORD says: Israel is my firstborn son, and I told you, 'Let my son go, so he may worship me.' But you refused to let him go; so I will kill your firstborn son" (Ex. 4:22–23). In other words, if you are going to keep and kill Israel, then measure for measure, the same will be done to you.

- This horrific plague caused a loud cry (*tze'akah*) to be heard throughout Egypt (Ex. 11:6), the very same cry that had been heard from the Israelites under their oppression (Ex. 2:23; 3:7, 9).

The First Passover

In the tenth and final plague, for the first time the Lord requires the Israelites to do something to be spared from the plague's harm. God gives them very specific instructions. On the tenth day of the month, every household is to select a one-year-old male lamb without defect, taking care of the lamb until the fourteenth day of the month when everyone must sacrifice the lamb at twilight, dipping hyssop into the blood and placing the blood on the sides and tops of the doorframes of their houses. Then no one can leave the house until morning. They must eat roasted lamb meat, bitter herbs, and bread made without leaven. The households must eat the meal in haste, with their cloak tucked into their belts, sandals on their feet, and staffs in hand. The plague of death will then "pass over" their homes, leaving alive the firstborn sons inside.

Moses tells the people:

> When you enter the land that the LORD will give you as he promised, observe this ceremony. And when your children ask you, "What does this ceremony mean to you?" then tell them, "It is the Passover sacrifice to the LORD, who passed over the houses of the Israelites in Egypt and spared our homes when he struck down the Egyptians." (Ex. 12:25–27)

Every detail of the first Passover meal is intentional, causing the Israelites to never forget God's deliverance.

The Miracle at the Sea

After the death of his firstborn son, Pharaoh finally lets the Israelites leave. But alas, Pharaoh's heart becomes hardened once again. He readies six hundred chariots and pursues the Israelites into the wilderness.

With Pharaoh and his army closing in, Israel comes to a dead end at the *yam suf*, which means "sea of reeds." (Though sometimes translated as the "Red Sea," the location of the sea in Exodus is unknown.) The people cry out to Moses, "Was it because there were no graves in Egypt that you brought us to the desert to die?" (Ex. 14:11). Moses seems to be stuck in reeds once again, this time with a people who, after a lifetime of slavery and oppression, find it difficult to trust the Lord.

Moses instructs them, "Do not be afraid. Stand firm and you will see the deliverance the LORD will bring you today. The Egyptians you see today you will never see again. The LORD will fight for you; you need only to be still" (Ex. 14:13–14).

God's pillars of cloud and fire move and stand between the armies of Israel and Egypt, bringing darkness to one side but light to the other. With the Egyptians held back by God, Moses stretches out his hand over the sea as the Lord divides it, allowing the Israelites to walk through on dry ground, with a wall of water on the right and left. God's separating of the chaotic waters is an image that harkens back to the creation account in Genesis 1. Through these waters, Israel is reborn.

Under Pharaoh's orders, his army pursues the people, but it becomes clear, even to the army, that God is fighting for Israel. The walls of the sea are released and the entire army is destroyed. Just as the waters of the Nile took the lives of the Hebrew baby boys, these waters take the lives of the pursuing army. It is this final miracle by the mighty hand of God that causes the Israelites to begin to trust: "The people feared the LORD and put their trust in him and in Moses his servant" (Ex. 14:31).

Exodus 15:1–18 records the song sung by Moses and Miriam, "Song of the Sea," which celebrates God's victory and the reasons why the people's trust is warranted. (This song is one of the oldest pieces of poetry in the Bible.)

After the crossing of the sea, Miriam, a prophet and sister of Aaron and Moses, takes a tambourine (timbrel) in hand. In the Song of the Sea, the women join her in dancing with their own tambourines, and together they declare, "Sing to the LORD, for he is highly exalted. Both horse and driver he has hurled into the sea" (Ex. 15:21).

If you had to flee your lifelong home, bringing with you only what you could carry, what would you grab? Food, water, clothing, money? For the Israelites leaving Egypt, whatever they brought with them had to be carried on their own backs or by their livestock for an unimaginable journey across difficult desert terrain. Miriam had the foresight to pack her tambourine. She brought an instrument of joy! She was prepared to celebrate and proclaim God's deliverance.

Miriam again lives up to her name, bringing forth rebellious joy, even in the face of bitter slavery and fear. Through the Song of the Sea, Moses, Miriam, and all the people declare that God's kingdom is eternal, greater than Pharaoh or any earthly empire that was or ever will be.

Life Application Questions

1. The Hebrew word *yad* ("hand") is repeated multiple times in Exodus 14 (see verses 16, 21, 26, 27, 30, 31). In what ways do you see God's mighty hand working in the world today?

2. In the end, the Hebrew slaves are delivered from oppression, but this comes only after much death, pain, and destruction. What do you think is the relationship between justice and suffering today?

3. What does the hardening of Pharaoh's heart mean? What might a hard heart look like nowadays?

4. The Israelites celebrated their freedom through song and dance. In what ways do you celebrate God's deliverance in your life?

5. The annual Passover retells the exodus account so that generations to come will always remember God's deliverance. Have you told your testimony of how the Lord saved you? Who in your life might need to hear your story?

Notes

5
GOD
COVENANTS

The Ten Commandments

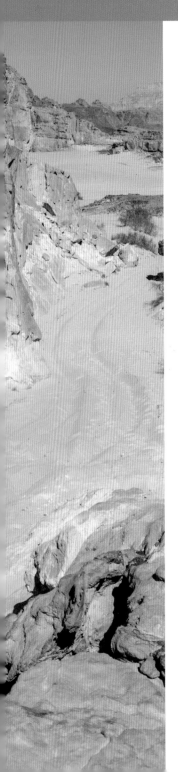

After the powerful display of God's sovereignty at the crossing of the sea, the people of God have finally escaped the land of their oppression. They travel for forty days through the Sinai Peninsula to arrive at the same mountain where God had promised Moses one year earlier at the burning bush that Israel would worship God.

If this were a movie, this would be the ending, right? The people free at last. Cue the uplifting music and roll the credits!

But there's much more to the story. Exodus is not just an account about the Hebrews being set free. It is not only a story about *freedom from*, but it is also a story of *freedom for*. True freedom cannot be found only in escaping from evil; there must be something more.

In the wilderness, however, the people begin to doubt, hesitate, grumble, and ultimately break trust with the Lord. Can the relationship between the people and the God who has just freed them be for something more, or will their relationship crumble in the desert? This is the question at the heart of this next part of the exodus story.

Read It

Key Bible Passage

For this session, read Exodus 19:1–20:21.

Optional Reading

Exodus chapters 24, 32, and 34

"Mount Sinai was covered with smoke, because the LORD descended on it in fire."

EXODUS 19:18

Know It

1. In Exodus 19, how many times does Moses climb up and down Mount Sinai? What does this tell you about Moses's commitment to God?

2. Why do you think God was so insistent about putting limits around the mountain?

3. The mountain was filled with thunder, lightning, fire, and smoke. If you had been there, what might you have felt or thought about this phenomenon?

Explore It

Where Was Mount Sinai?

Though the Bible provides a fairly detailed list of the Israelites' movements from Goshen to the mountain in Sinai (Ex. 12:37–19:2; Num. 33:1–15), many of the locations were uninhabited sites and identifying them in both ancient and modern contexts can be very difficult, if not impossible. Yet we are not totally in the dark. Bible scholars have done their best to piece together the information found in Scripture along with archaeological sites and have proposed several options for the route of the exodus and the location of Mount Sinai.

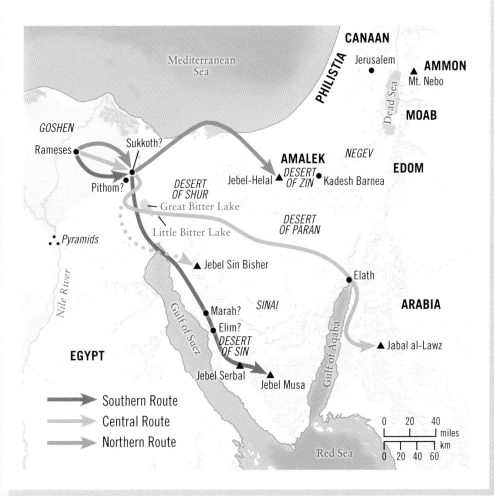

Southern Route: If the Israelites took this route, they would have left Goshen and headed south through the Sinai Peninsula. Traditionally, Mount Sinai is located near the southern tip of the peninsula at Jebel Musa, though some suggest it may lie a little farther north, near the Desert of Sin at Jebel Serbal.

Central Route: Following this route, the Israelites would have taken a more central path across the middle of the Sinai Peninsula. Mount Sinai may have been located at Jabal al-Lawz in Arabia. Potential problems with this view include the harshness of the route (lack of water) and the amount of time it would have taken to reach the crossing point into Arabia. Alternately, Mount Sinai may have been located at Jebel Sin Bisher in the Sinai Peninsula.

Northern Route: According to this route, the Israelites headed north, with Mount Sinai in the northwestern area of the Sinai Peninsula at Jebel-Helal. However, this option does not take into account that Scripture says God led Israel away from the Philistines located along the Mediterranean coast (Ex. 13:17–18). It is also inconsistent with the eleven-day journey mentioned in Deuteronomy 1:2.

The Covenant

At Sinai, the Lord descends upon the mountain in fire and smoke, and he calls Moses to ascend the mountain to meet him. He instructs Moses to give this message to Israel:

> You yourselves have seen what I did to Egypt, and how I carried you on eagles' wings and brought you to myself. Now if you obey me fully and keep my covenant, then out of all nations you will be my treasured possession. Although the whole earth is mine, you will be for me a kingdom of priests and a holy nation. (Ex. 19:4–6)

God reminds Israel that he has already saved them. They have already been rescued, redeemed, and delivered from slavery and oppression. The question is: how will Israel respond? Will they covenant with God and become his treasured possession, a priestly kingdom, and a holy nation?

It's important to note that the keeping of the covenant was not required for the Israelites' deliverance, salvation, and rescue from Egypt. God had already done that for them. Sometimes we think that salvation in the Old Testament needed to be earned through obedience and good works. Nothing could be further from the truth. God has always been a God of loving faithfulness who rescues and redeems people.

Mount Sinai

The traditional Mount Sinai, called Jebel Musa (the Mountain of Moses), is in southern Sinai and rises approximately 7,500 feet (2,285 m) above sea level. Jebel Musa has served as the attested location of Mount Sinai since the late fourth century AD, with a monastery built there in the sixth century to protect the traditional site of the burning bush.

St. Catherine's monastery at Mount Sinai (Jebel Musa)

When Moses returns to the people, sharing with them what God has said, they answer as one: "We will do everything the LORD has said" (Ex. 19:8). (A similar response by the people is found in Exodus 24:7.) Israel agrees to God's covenant and commandments even before they hear them. We often want to know all the details from God before we say yes, but here we see the people's joy at receiving God's commands, even before they knew what they were.

Now that both parties agree to the covenant, preparations for the ceremony are underway. Moses's role is affirmed, Israel is purified for three days, and a boundary is set around the holy mountain since it served as God's dwelling place. On the third day, there is thunder, lightning, a thick cloud on the mountain, and a blast of a trumpet (a ram's horn, or shofar) so loud that it causes all the people to tremble. The mountain shakes violently, the trumpet blast grows louder, and

Shofar

as Moses speaks, God answers in the thunder. (The Hebrew word for thunder, *kol*, can also mean "voice.") The covenant ceremony begins with the words, "I am the LORD your God, who brought you out of the land of Egypt, out of the house of slavery; you shall have no other gods before me" (Ex. 20:2–3 NRSVUE). The opening lines set the stage for everything to follow.

By using the same language used for entering into a marriage bond, God establishes his relationship with Israel, demanding faithfulness and loyalty, forsaking all others (Ex. 20:4–7). Earlier, in Exodus 6:7, God says, "I will *take you* as my own people," and Exodus 19:4–6 includes the phrase, "*brought you* to myself." Both phrases are used in the Old Testament to describe the marriage relationship between a husband and wife.

This imagery was not lost on ancient Israel or the biblical authors: "Do not worship any other god, for the LORD, whose name is Jealous, is a jealous God" (Ex. 34:14). When Israel bowed down to other gods, they were accused of adultery (Jer. 3:6–9; Hos. 2:1–13). When the prophets sought to bring the people back to the Lord, they reminded the Israelites of when, as a young bride of the Lord, they wandered in the wilderness (Jer. 2:1–3; Hos. 2:14–20; see also John 3:29; Rev. 21:2).

In the exodus narrative, the Ten Commandments are less like a list of ten do's and don'ts and more like covenantal marriage vows, gladly entered into by God and the people he rescued.

The Two Tablets

The tablets of the Ten Commandments were written on both sides and were the work of God. The two tablets are most often depicted as one tablet listing commandments one through five and the other tablet listing six through ten—as if God cannot write small enough to get all the commandments on one tablet! It is more likely, however, that each tablet was a copy of the other. (Just like today, when purchasing a home, car, or even a gym membership, two copies of a contract are provided, one for each party.) The practice of duplicating the full text of an agreement can be seen in ancient suzerain vassal treaties—common among the Hittites, Egyptians, Assyrians, and Israelites— in which a covenant is made between a greater (suzerain) and a lesser (vassal) party.

Cuneiform tablet of
Egyptian-Hittite peace treaty

The Golden Calf

Tragically, while Moses is up on the mountain for some time, Israel begins to lose heart. They turn to Aaron and ask him to make them an image of the God who brought them up out of Egypt. Aaron collects gold pilfered from the Egyptians, puts it into a fire and, in his retelling later, "out comes this calf!" (Ex. 32:24). The people sacrifice on the altar in front of the golden calf, bow down to the idol, and engage in revelry. On the wedding night, Israel commits adultery, breaking the first two commandments!

Things had turned. The Lord tells Moses, "Go down at once! Your people, whom you brought up out of the land of Egypt, have acted perversely.... Let me alone that my wrath may burn hot against them" (Ex. 32:7, 10 NRSVUE). A true prophet, Moses intercedes on behalf of the people by reminding God of his covenantal promises and ultimately playing to God's reputation by saying, "But what will they say about you in Egypt?" (Ex. 32:12). God relents.

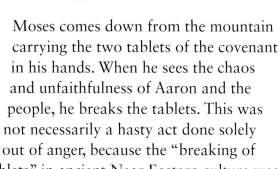

Small bronze bull, Israel, 12th century BC

Moses comes down from the mountain carrying the two tablets of the covenant in his hands. When he sees the chaos and unfaithfulness of Aaron and the people, he breaks the tablets. This was not necessarily a hasty act done solely out of anger, because the "breaking of tablets" in ancient Near Eastern culture was a way of signifying the end of an agreement, rendering a covenant null and void—much like we'd say today "tearing up a contract." Israel had broken their marriage vows, so Moses is calling off the wedding.

Moses takes the golden calf, grinds it into a powder, and makes the Israelites drink it. (This is similar to the ordeal of a wife accused of unfaithfulness found in Numbers 5:11–31.) He then calls the Levites to rally with him, and they go through the camp, killing about 3,000 people! On the occasion of the giving of God's commands, there is betrayal, faithlessness, adultery, and death.

This must be the end of the covenant relationship, right? No, God tells Moses to try again: "Chisel out two stone tablets like the first ones" (Ex. 34:1). Moses obeys, and he ascends Mount Sinai once again, and God descends in a cloud, proclaiming mercy towards his unfaithful people: "The LORD, the LORD, the compassionate and gracious God, slow to anger, abounding in love and faithfulness, maintaining love to thousands, and forgiving wickedness, rebellion and sin" (Ex. 34:6–7). The people were punished for breaking their vows, but they were not annihilated nor ultimately abandoned (see Ex. 32:35; 33:14).

God is faithful when we are not. God forgives when we do not deserve it. And God will never, ever give up on us.

Live It

How would our own lives be different if we read the Ten Commandments, not as a list of ways we haven't measured up, but instead with the tone and mindset of marriage vows between two parties that love and are committed to one another? God's commands are not legalistic burdens or ways in which we secure salvation. (Remember, God gave the Israelites his commands *after* he delivered them from Egypt.) God's instructions bring us joy, hope, peace, and stability. When we steal from a neighbor, trust dies between us. When we cheat, lie, or cause harm, the fabric of society begins to unravel; safety, security, and hope fray.

At the end of his life—and in the longest sermon ever—Moses explains that the people have two choices: "I have set before you life and death, blessings and curses. Now choose life, so that you and your children may live and that you may love the LORD your God, listen to his voice, and hold fast to him" (Deut. 30:19–20). Choose life, for the Lord is your life. If we love God, we will strive to keep his commandments (John 14:15). Being chosen to covenant with God is not a burden but a privilege and a blessing.

Life Application Questions

1. In Exodus, God's presence is made known through fire and smoke, thunder and lightning, a pillar of clouds, and the sound of trumpets. What kind of imagery most resonates with you when you think of God's presence?

2. How might looking at the Ten Commandments through the lens of covenant vows change one's perspective on the purpose of the commandments?

3. Do you think all of the Ten Commandments should be followed by Christians today? Why or why not?

4. Why do you think Aaron and the people made the golden calf, especially after everything they had seen God do in Egypt?

5. What are some "golden calves" that people look toward today? What harmful things are you tempted to turn to in times of doubt?

Notes

Notes

GOD DWELLS

The Tabernacle

God Dwells

Why did God choose the Israelites to be his holy people, to rescue them from slavery and to covenant with them? Were they the most righteous amongst the nations? No, they did not even know God's name or have his commandments before he brought them out of Egypt. Was it because they were so numerous that God thought it good to choose such a large population? No, they were "the fewest of all the peoples" (Deut. 7:7). Instead, as Moses explained, "The LORD loved you and kept the oath he swore to your ancestors that he brought you out with a mighty hand and redeemed you from the land of slavery" (Deut. 7:8).

It was through God's covenantal faithfulness to and love of our ancestors that the entire world would be blessed. We can see this all throughout the Bible: God is seeking to be with his creation whom he loves. God is trying to get us all back to the garden of Eden, when, in the cool of the day, he walked among us and *dwelt* with us (see Gen. 3:8).

Read It

Key Bible Passage

For this session, read Exodus 29:44–46 and 40:1–38.

Optional Reading

Deuteronomy 34:1–12

"The cloud covered the tent of meeting, and the glory of the Lord filled the tabernacle."

EXODUS 40:34

1. Of all the tabernacle items listed in Exodus 40, which one caught your attention or sparked your curiosity? Why?

2. What was the purpose of the cloud covering the tabernacle in Exodus 40:34–38?

3. What does Exodus 40 reveal about the relationship between God and Moses, and also between God and the people?

God's Tent of Meeting

Israel and God covenanted with one another at Mount Sinai. So next, it is time to live with each other. How will God do this? Well, just as the Israelites live in tents, the Lord will dwell in a tent (though a much fancier one). Starting in Exodus 25, God instructs the people to build him a movable tabernacle and pitch it in the center of their encampment in the wilderness. God will live at the center, traveling with them and being found by them. Of course the people understood that the God of the universe could not be held in any tent or building or other location, but the tabernacle would be the place where God had agreed to meet with them. Indeed, one of the names for the tabernacle is "tent of meeting."

Since the incident with the sneaky snake in the garden of Eden, God's people had been living in exile, kicked out from the home God created for them. After Eden came violence, a great flood, and a tower of hubris. Everything went sideways, until God called a man named Abraham and made a covenant with him; and not only with him, but also with all his descendants, as numerous as the stars in the sky and the sand on the seashore. This covenant was God's way of blessing every person on earth (Gen. 12:3). It was the beginning of God's rescue plan to once again be with us— to dwell with us.

In Exodus 29, God states his intentions plainly: "I will consecrate the tent of meeting.... I will dwell among the Israelites and be their God. They will know that I am the LORD their God, who brought them out of Egypt so that I might dwell among them. I am the LORD their God" (Ex. 29:44–46). In Hebrew, verse 45 reads literally, "I will dwell *in* [*b'toch*] Israel." How incredible! God seems to be finding ways to get us back to the garden so that he can dwell among us, to "tabernacle" among us, and be found by humanity.

The account of the creation of the world is only given a few paragraphs in Genesis, while the account of the tabernacle takes up more than ten chapters in the book of Exodus. The creation of the tabernacle is told twice: the first account details the instructions (Ex. 25–31), and the second details its construction (Ex. 36–39). This echoes the two creation accounts in Genesis 1 and 2. The phrase "The LORD said to Moses" appears seven times in the tabernacle instructions: Ex. 25:1; 30:11; 30:17; 30:22; 30:34; 31:1; 31:12. The seventh time concludes with God's command to observe the Sabbath, the day of rest. This structure is similar to the six days of creation in Genesis which concludes with the seventh day, when God rested. (For more parallels between Genesis and Exodus, compare Ex. 39:32 with Gen. 2:1, 3; Ex. 39:43 with Gen. 1:31; Ex. 40:33 with Gen. 2:2.) The creation of the tabernacle is, in a way, a re-creation that God is bringing into the world.

The creation narrative in Genesis does not just tell us that something happened, but also that it *happens*. Behold, God is doing a new thing! God is still creating. God called order out of chaos, separated the waters—and now, with echoes of Eden, God is still bringing forth new creation. Human disobedience removed us from the best of creation, but God still longs to be with us, to dwell with us.

Called to Holiness

The courtyard of the tabernacle was a rectangle. When divided into two squares, each contained at its center an item of special interest:

- At the center of the Outer Court, people made offerings at the altar as a way for the people to draw near to God. (The word for offering in Hebrew, *korban*, is derived from the word *karov*, which means "to draw near.")

- At the center of the Inner Court, God's presence rested on the ark of the covenant, as God drew near to the people.

Built into the design and centered in the religious practice of the tabernacle is the ability for God and God's people to be with one another in this new creation. Still today, God is reaching out to us and we are reaching out for God.

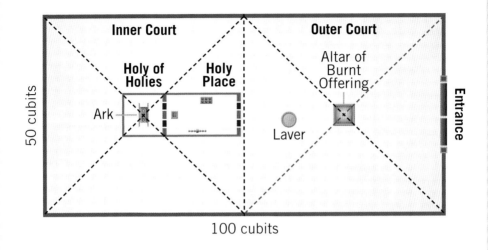

Remember back to the covenant ceremony at Mount Sinai. There were two tablets of the covenant, one copy for Israel and the other for God. After the tabernacle was constructed, both tablets were stored in the ark of the covenant. God and the people kept their copies together in the same place, because they dwelt together: "For what other great nation has a god so near to it as the LORD our God is whenever we call to him?" (Deut. 4:7 NRSVUE).

No wonder Israel was called to live differently from the world. As they went about, they were to carry God's holy presence as a light to the nations. Again and again throughout the Bible, God says, in so many different ways, "Be holy, because I am holy" (Lev. 11:45). Similar perhaps to a parent's response when a child begs, "But all the other kids' parents are letting them do it!" It didn't matter what all the other nations were doing. God's children, as his holy nation, his kingdom of priests, were expected to be different. This was not legalism but instead was a covenantal relationship and response meant to shine God's light into a dark world. Ancient Israel was to serve as the caretakers of God's dwelling place, the place of reconciliation and shalom between the divine and the creation.

In the pages of Exodus, and in the books that follow—Leviticus, Numbers, and Deuteronomy—we see that Moses and the Israelites didn't always live up to their high calling. Like us today, they sinned, grumbled, rebelled, and doubted God's goodness. And also like us, they experienced judgment, consequences, restoration, forgiveness, and mercy. In fact, as a consequence of their rebellion, an entire generation, including Moses, was kept from entering the promised land. Though even this judgment seems to be a mercy as those Israelites who had experienced oppression and slavery in Egypt were not permitted to bring that mindset into the new land. It died with them in the desert.

Conclusion

The book of Deuteronomy concludes the narrative of Israel's desert wanderings. With all the people assembled on the plains just east of the Jordan River across from the promised land, Moses climbs a mountain one last time. From the top of Mount Nebo, God gives Moses a view of the land—the place for which he had led the people out of Egypt. "Moses was a hundred and twenty years old when he died, yet his eyes were not weak nor his strength gone" (Deut. 34:7). It would be the next generation, led by Moses's successor Joshua, who would enter Canaan and find a home in the land God promised to Abraham's descendants.

Live It

If God were to dwell separately and apart from people, the need for human holiness would not be as great. But because God longs to be here with us, we must live in a way that can receive his presence in our midst. In the New Testament, the Christian community is described as being a spiritual temple, the holy dwelling place of God's Spirit (Eph. 2:19–22). Together, believers are to become a sacred environment acceptable to God, reflecting the holiness of his heavenly realm here on earth and carrying the presence of Christ into the world.

That is a high bar indeed! And God knows that we will not be able to avoid sinning; we will sin intentionally and unintentionally. In the wilderness, God provided the sacrifices and ceremonies that took place at the tabernacle as a means for atoning for sin and restoring holiness. God has always provided ways to rebuild relationship with him after humans have sinned. We are not defined forever by our sin, but instead we are given beautiful ways to start again, embracing our identity as forgiven and clean.

There is responsibility on our part for the great blessing of having God in our midst. Our response should be to live in such a way that the Lord *can* dwell among us. We must be a holy people, remaining faithful to the one true God. We must not cheat, murder, envy, lie, steal, or commit adultery, but we must care for the stranger, the orphan, and the widow—for the Lord our God is holy (1 Peter 1:14–15).

The book of Exodus closes with this incredibly awe-inspiring, miraculous statement: "Then the cloud covered the tent of meeting and the glory of the Lord filled the tabernacle" (Ex. 40:34). May we tell this story all over the world, again and again, because our God still hears, still rescues, still forgives, still loves, still calls us, and still longs to dwell with us.

Life Application Questions

1. Read John 1:14. Depending on the translation, Jesus (the Word) "lived," "dwelled," or "tabernacled" among us. In light of what you've learned in Exodus, what does this mean to you?

2. How can the church today carry the presence of Christ into the world? Give some specific examples.

3. Read Revelation 21:3. How confident are you that one day all things will be set right and we will once again walk with God in the new creation?

4. When in your life have you strongly felt God's presence, him walking closely with you?

5. Looking back over this study of the exodus, what is one thing that God has shown you through this experience?

Notes

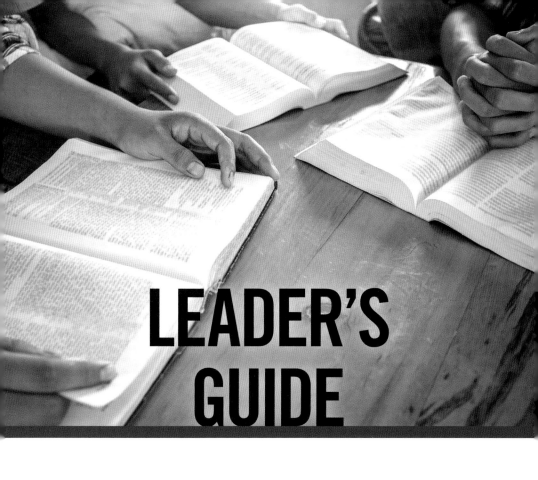

LEADER'S GUIDE

"*Encourage one another and build each other up.*"

1 THESSALONIANS 5:11

Leader's Guide

Congratulations! You've either decided to lead a Bible study, or you're thinking hard about it. Guess what? God does big things through small groups. When his people gather together, open his Word, and invite his Spirit to work, their lives are changed!

Do you feel intimidated yet?

Be comforted by this: even the great apostle Paul felt "in over his head" at times. When he went to Corinth to help people grasp God's truth, he admitted he was overwhelmed: "I came to you in weakness with great fear and trembling" (1 Corinthians 2:3). Later he wondered, "Who is adequate for such a task as this?" (2 Corinthians 2:16 NLT).

Feelings of inadequacy are normal; every leader has them. What's more, they're actually healthy. They keep us dependent on the Lord. It is in our times of greatest weakness that God works most powerfully. The Lord assured Paul, "My grace is sufficient for you, for my power is made perfect in weakness" (2 Corinthians 12:9).

The Goal

What is the goal of a Bible study group? Listen as the apostle Paul speaks to Christians:

- "Oh, my dear children! I feel as if I'm going through labor pains for you again, and they will continue until *Christ is fully developed in your lives*" (Galatians 4:19 NLT, emphasis added).

- "For God knew his people in advance, and he chose them *to become like his Son*" (Romans 8:29 NLT, emphasis added).

Do you see it? God's ultimate goal for us is that we would become like Jesus Christ. This means a Bible study is not about filling our heads with more information. Rather, it is about undergoing transformation. We study and apply God's truth so that it will reshape our hearts and minds, and so that over time, we will become more and more like Jesus.

Paul said, "The purpose of my instruction is that all believers would be filled with love that comes from a pure heart, a clear conscience, and genuine faith" (1 Timothy 1:5 NLT).

This isn't about trying to "master the Bible." No, we're praying that God's Word will master us, and through humble submission to its authority, we'll be changed from the inside out.

Your Role

Many group leaders experience frustration because they confuse their role with God's role. Here's the truth: God alone knows our deep hang-ups and hurts. Only he can save a soul, heal a heart, fix a life. It is God who rescues people from depression, addictions, bitterness, guilt, and shame. We Bible study leaders need to realize that *we can't do any of those things.*

So what can we do? More than we think!

- We can pray.

- We can trust God to work powerfully.

- We can obey the Spirit's promptings.

- We can prepare for group gatherings.

- We can keep showing up faithfully.

With group members:

- We can invite, remind, encourage, and love.

- We can ask good questions and then listen attentively.

- We can gently speak tough truths.

- We can celebrate with those who are happy and weep with those who are sad.

- We can call and text and let them know we've got their back.

But we can never do the things that only the Almighty can do.

- We can't play the Holy Spirit in another person's life.

- We can't be in charge of outcomes.

- We can't force God to work according to our timetables.

And one more important reminder: besides God's role and our role, group members also have a key role to play in this process. If they don't show up, prepare, or open their hearts to God's transforming truth, no life change will take place. We're not called to manipulate or shame, pressure or arm twist. We're not to blame if members don't make progress—and we don't get the credit when they do. We're mere instruments in the hands of God.

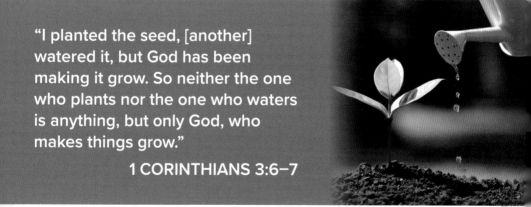

"I planted the seed, [another] watered it, but God has been making it grow. So neither the one who plants nor the one who waters is anything, but only God, who makes things grow."

1 CORINTHIANS 3:6–7

Leader Myths and Truths

Many people assume that a Bible study leader should:

- Be a Bible scholar.

- Be a dynamic communicator.

- Have a big, fancy house to meet in.

- Have it all together—no doubts, bad habits, or struggles.

These are myths—even outright lies of the enemy!

Here's the truth:

- God is looking for humble Bible students, not scholars.

- You're not signing up to give lectures, you're agreeing to facilitate discussions.

- You don't need a palace, just a place where you can have uninterrupted discussions. (Perhaps one of your group members will agree to host your study.)

- Nobody has it all together. We are all in process. We are all seeking to work out "our salvation with fear and trembling" (Philippians 2:12).

As long as your desire is that Jesus be Lord of your life, God will use you!

- You want to wow others with your biblical knowledge.

  "Love . . . does not boast, it is not proud"
  (1 Corinthians 13:4).

- You're seeking a hidden personal gain or profit.

  "We do not peddle the word of God for profit"
  (2 Corinthians 2:17).

- You want to tell people how wrong they are.

  "Do not condemn" (Romans 2:1).

- You want to fix or rescue people.

  "It is God who works in you to will and to act"
  (Philippians 2:13).

- You're being pressured to do it.

  "Am I now trying to win the approval of
  human beings, or of God?" (Galatians 1:10).

A Few Do's

✔ Pray for your group.

Are you praying for your group members regularly? It is the most important thing a leader can do for his or her group.

✔ Ask for help.

If you're new at leading, spend time with an experienced group leader and pick his or her brain.

✔ Encourage members to prepare.

Challenge participants to read the Bible passages and the material in their study guides, and to answer and reflect on the study questions during the week prior to meeting.

✔ Discuss the group guidelines.

Go over important guidelines with your group at the first session, and again as needed if new members join the group in later sessions. See the *Group Guidelines* at the end of this leader's guide.

✔ Share the load.

Don't be a one-person show. Ask for volunteers. Let group members host the meeting, arrange for snacks, plan socials, lead group prayer times, and so forth. The old saying is true: Participants become boosters; spectators become critics.

✔ Be flexible.

If a group member shows up in crisis, it is okay to stop and take time to surround the hurting brother or sister with love. Provide a safe place for sharing. Listen and pray for his or her needs.

✔ Be kind.

Remember, there's a story—often a heart-breaking one—behind every face. This doesn't *excuse* bad or disruptive behavior on the part of group members, but it might *explain* it.

A Few Don'ts

✘ Don't "wing it."

Although these sessions are designed to require minimum preparation, read each one ahead of time. Highlight the questions you feel are especially important for your group to spend time on.

✘ Don't feel ashamed to say, "I don't know."

Disciple means "learner," not "know-it-all."

✘ Don't feel the need to "dump the truck."

You don't have to say everything you know. There is always next week. A little silence during group discussion time, that's fine. Let members wrestle with questions.

✘ Don't put members on the spot.

Invite others to share and pray, but don't pressure them. Give everyone an opportunity to participate. People will open up on their own time as they learn to trust the group.

✘ Don't go down "rabbit trails."

Be careful not to let one person dominate the time or for the discussion to go down the gossip road. At the same time, don't short-circuit those occasions when the Holy Spirit is working in your group members' lives and therefore they *need* to share a lot.

✘ Don't feel pressure to cover every question.

Better to have a robust discussion of four questions than a superficial conversation of ten.

✘ Don't go long.

Encourage good discussion, but don't be afraid to "rope 'em back in" when needed. Start and end on time. If you do this from the beginning, you'll avoid the tendency of group members to arrive later and later as the season goes on.

How to Use This Study Guide

Many group members have busy lives—dealing with long work hours, childcare, and a host of other obligations. These sessions are designed to be as simple and straightforward as possible to fit into a busy schedule. Nevertheless, encourage group members to set aside some time during the week (even if it's only a little) to pray, read the key Bible passage, and respond to questions in this study guide. This will make the group discussion and experience much more rewarding for everyone.

Each session contains four parts.

Read It

The *Key Bible Passage* is the portion of Scripture everyone should read during the week before the group meeting. The group can read it together at the beginning of the session as well.

The *Optional Reading* is for those who want to dig deeper and read lengthier Bible passages on their own during the week.

Know It

This section encourages participants to reflect on the Bible passage they've just read. Here, the goal is to interact with the biblical text and grasp what it says. (We'll get into practical application later.)

Explore It

Here group members can find background information with charts and visuals to help them understand the Bible passage and the topic more deeply. They'll move beyond the text itself and see how it connects to other parts of Scripture and the historical and cultural context.

Live It

Finally, participants will examine how God's Word connects to their lives. There are application questions for group discussion or personal reflection, practical ideas to apply what they've learned from God's Word, and a closing thought and/or prayer. (Remember, you don't have to cover all the questions or everything in this section during group time. Focus on what's most important for your group.)

Celebrate!

Here's an idea: Have a plan for celebrating your time together after the last session of this Bible study. Do something special after your gathering time, or plan a separate celebration for another time and place. Maybe someone in your group has the gift of hospitality—let them use their gifting and organize the celebration.

	30-MINUTE SESSION	60-MINUTE SESSION
READ IT	Open in prayer and read the *Key Bible Passage.* 5 minutes	Open in prayer and read the *Key Bible Passage.* 5 minutes
KNOW IT	Ask: "What stood out to you from this Bible passage?" 5 minutes	Ask: "What stood out to you from this Bible passage?" 5 minutes
EXPLORE IT	Encourage group members to read this section on their own, but don't spend group time on it. Move on to the life application questions.	Ask: "What did you find new or helpful in the *Explore It* section? What do you still have questions about?" 10 minutes
LIVE IT	Members voluntarily share their answers to 3 or 4 of the life application questions. 15 minutes	Members voluntarily share their answers to the life application questions. 25 minutes
PRAYER & CLOSING	Conclude with a brief prayer. 5 minutes	Share prayer requests and praise reports. Encourage the group to pray for each other in the coming week. Conclude with a brief prayer. 15 minutes

Open in prayer and read the *Key Bible Passage.*

5 minutes

- Ask: "What stood out to you from this Bible passage?"
- Then go over the *Know It* questions as a group.

10 minutes

- Ask: "What did you find new or helpful in the *Explore It* section? What do you still have questions about?"
- Here, the leader can add information found while preparing for the session.
- If there are questions or a worksheet in this section, go over those as a group.

20 minutes

- Members voluntarily share their answers to the life application questions.
- Wrap up this time with a closing thought or suggestions for how to put into practice in the coming week what was just learned from God's Word.

30 minutes

- Share prayer requests and praise reports.
- Members voluntarily pray during group time about the requests and praises shared.
- Encourage the group to pray for each other in the coming week.

25 minutes

Group Guidelines

This group is about discovering God's truth, supporting each other, and finding growth in our new life in Christ. To reach these goals, a group needs a few simple guidelines that everyone should follow for the group to stay healthy and for trust to develop.

1. **Everyone agrees to make group time a priority.**
   We understand that there are work, health, and family issues that come up. So if there is an emergency or schedule conflict that cannot be avoided, be sure to let someone know that you can't make it that week. This may seem like a small thing, but it makes a big difference to your other group members.

2. **What is said in the group stays in the group.**
   Accept it now: we are going to share some personal things. Therefore, the group must be a safe and confidential place to share.

3. **Don't be judgmental, even if you strongly disagree.**
   Listen first, and contribute your perspective only as needed. Remember, you don't fully know someone else's story. Take this advice from James: "Be quick to listen, slow to speak, and slow to become angry" (James 1:19).

4. **Be patient with one another.**
   We are all in process, and some of us are hurting and struggling more than others. Don't expect bad habits or attitudes to disappear overnight.

5. **Everyone participates.**
   It may take time to learn how to share, but as you develop a trust toward the other group members, take the chance.

If you struggle in any of these areas, ask God's help for growth, and ask the group to help hold you accountable. Remember, you're all growing together.

Notes

ROSE VISUAL BIBLE STUDIES
6-Session Study Guides for Personal or Group Use

THE BOOK OF JAMES
Find out how to cultivate a living faith through six tests of faith.

THE TABERNACLE
Discover how each item of the tabernacle foreshadowed Jesus.

THE ARMOR OF GOD
Dig deep into Ephesians 6 and learn the meaning of each piece of the armor.

THE LIFE OF PAUL
See how the apostle Paul persevered through trials and proclaimed the gospel.

JOURNEY TO THE RESURRECTION
Renew your heart and mind as you engage in spiritual practices. Perfect for Easter.

I AM
Know the seven powerful claims of Christ from the gospel of John.

THE TWELVE DISCIPLES
Learn about the twelve men Jesus chose to be his disciples.

PROVERBS
Gain practical, godly wisdom from the book of Proverbs.

WOMEN OF THE BIBLE: OLD TESTAMENT
Journey through six inspiring stories of women of courage and wisdom.

WOMEN OF THE BIBLE: NEW TESTAMENT
See women's impact in the ministry of Jesus and the early church.

THE LORD'S PRAYER
Deepen your prayer life with the seven petitions in the Lord's Prayer.

FRUIT OF THE SPIRIT
Explore the nine spiritual fruits.

PSALMS
Discover the wild beauty of praise.

THE EXODUS
Witness God's mighty acts in the exodus.

THE BOOK OF JOB
Explore questions about faith and suffering.

www.hendricksonrose.com